Neither do people light a lamp and put it under a bushel, but on a lamp stand; and it gives light unto all that are in the house. Let your light shine before men, that they may see your good works, and glorify your Father which is in heaven. Matthew 5:15-16.

The first poem I wrote was in the fourth grade at summer camp. I recall like it was yesterday the camp counselor telling me I had a gift. And that gift needed to be placed on a "lamp stand."

Growing up in a crowded apartment the youngest of eleven children, there was no such thing as privacy or having an opinion, or a voice, for that matter. Poetry became my outlet and my way of letting the world know I had a voice.

*Mary Marrero Tinajero*

PUSHING PAST PAIN

*Through Poetry*

# PUSHING PAST PAIN
# Through Poetry

## LOVE LETTERS
## TO
## MY FAMILY

### Mary M. Tinajero

XULON PRESS

Xulon Press Elite
2301 Lucien Way #415
Maitland, FL 32751
407.339.4217
www.xulonpress.com

Unless otherwise indicated, Scripture quotations taken
from the Holy Bible, New International Version (NIV).
Copyright © 1973, 1978, 1984, 2011 by Biblica, Inc.™.
Used by permission. All rights reserved.

Printed in the United States of America.

ISBN-13: 978-1-6305-0621-6

Poetry has been my form of expressing my innermost thoughts and feelings. They are my words when I cannot articulate them. The thoughts and feelings which my lips couldn't form when emotions made it difficult to communicate. *Pushing past pain through writing poetry* has been my salve, my medicine for the soul.

This book is dedicated to my loved ones: Charles, Andrew, Jennifer, Olivia, Violet, Louisa, my dear sisters who have been my rock, and my parents. This is my labor of love to those closest to my heart.

I thank God for giving me the gift which for so many years I have taken for granted. The poems have been written for family and friends during times of their lives they needed encouragement or hope. May it bless you, the reader, as well.

In Christ,
Mary Marrero Tinajero Thomas

I married my son's father in 1985. I truly believe people enter marriage believing it will last forever. Our marriage didn't last. The pain of divorce and loss was immense. This was my prayer to the Father:

Lord:

Why have I felt as though I have been in the outside looking in? The film of shame, guilt and brokenness have blinded my sight. The iniquity caused by my sin.

Lord, why do I feel the pain of bareness in my heart and in my soul? I can't remember feeling complete. I know I once did, oh so long ago.

Lord, why do I feel alone? I know that you love me and died on the cross for me so that one day I could make heaven my home.

Lord, come and heal my brokenness like no one else can. For I know there is no happiness in the things of this earthly realm and there is no grace in putting our faith in man.

Lord, come and speak to me as you did with Abraham, David and Paul. A word to heal my heart and me whole so I have no pain at all.

Lord, come and bless this broken heart, broken from the inside out. Heal me so I can testify to what you're all about.

Heal me, Lord. Heal this broken heart. Let me sing your praises, Lord, let me praise you and honor you through songs, dancing and shouts.

Touch me with your holiness so I can be free from my darkness and gloom. Make me rise from my man-made tomb. Make my life what you purposed for me when you placed me in my mother's womb.

Amen.

My son, Andrew Amador, was always my little shadow and my pride and joy. I always share with him that the day he was born is when I realized how much I was loved by God. That God in His infinite mercy would gift me with such a precious gift of life. A healthy, bouncing, black-haired, green-eyed treasure that would forever give me joy. I wrote this poem when my son was off to college.

# My Little Man

I can remember like yesterday, the little person who always wanted to hold my hand. Suddenly, time, like a thief, ran its course. My little green-eyed boy was now a college bound handsome man.

I can remember when all he wanted was to have me ride him on my back. My silly boy, no siblings to entertain him, I was his human toy.

I remember his hugs and kisses, never short on his affection or love. I thank God for him, my treasure, my darling, and joy, sent from above.

I remember rocking in my arms as he fell fast asleep. I sang his favorite Spanish lullaby and I prayed to God. "Keep my baby's sleep in perfect peace."

I remember his smile, his sweetness, his tender heart. The years, oh how they slip by so fast. Soon he will walk into the world to start his life and those little hands that grasped my hands so tight will soon unlock and part.

In all my life, I've been in awe of the gift God granted me in giving me my little man. He will always be my little boy and I will always be his most loyal fan.

I wrote this poem for Andrew's birthday. A mother's tribute to honor his right of passage to adulthood.

# Grown

How could it be that yesterday I held you for the first time? Ocean green eyes and raven black hair, this little snuggle bug was really mine. You were God's gift made from the seeds of love. My answer to prayer from our Lord above.

You found great joy in scaring me by bringing me bugs from the outside that you found where you played. You laughed out loud when I screamed in horror and dismay.

It was precious when you learned to play the guitar. You were my little Elvis Presley. My little movie star.

I remember how you would belt out in laughter any time I saw a mouse. You found it so funny when I screamed in horror if we found one scurrying inside the house.

You have always made me proud in everything you do. You're a man after God's own heart and the apple of my eyes too.

So, on this day of your birthday, my thoughts of you are really nothing new. Because I thank God for you each morning and I thank him that he loved me so much that he gifted me with you!!

*Momma*

The Lord gave me a second chance at love. Charles endeared me to his loving and generous heart. His love for family and sense of humor won me over. As mutual dog lovers, he stole my heart forever when I met his dog, sweet Fidel. We would marry in a quiet, private ceremony in our pastor's office at church. Charles wakes up each morning without an alarm clock. The sun shining through our windows is his gentle wake up call. I wrote this one morning as he deeply slept beside me.

# The Morning Sun

He loves the morning sun kissing his face. God's simple greeting of love and grace.

All day long, he whispers underneath his breath, that wisdom and goodness guide him through life's trials and tests.

And while he is merely a man, perfection unachieved, he upholds his moral compass, for mortal man he refuses to please.

His spirit breathes joy, laughter and love. Our father in heaven smiles and showers his approval from above.

The morning sun kisses his ebony face. Wake up, my son, lift your sword. I love you. Take your rightful place.

*Mary*

Bessie was an elder at our church. For some lovely stroke of fate, this beautiful woman chose to take me under her wings as a new member of the church. I accepted the invitation with gladness. You see, I was a rarity at our church. It was a huge megachurch with predominantly black members who didn't take kindly to a mixed-race couple like Charles and me. She would be that shining light and sweet encounter each Sunday morning. Her beautiful and loving spirit was a huge reminder of Godly love and acceptance.

# Gardenia

Your beauty reminds me of my favorite flower,
the Gardenia.
Lovely and elegant, the petals of silky velvet,
strong amidst the spring and summer showers.

Your kindness, as though sent from God above.
Your face, shines like a flint, emanates the Father's love.

The goodness of life shines on your gorgeous ebony face.
I can see in your eye's God's beauty and grace.

Woman of God, you remind me of the most lovely and
delicate flower, the Gardenia.

In its purity and beauty after a heavenly shower.

Thank you for blessing me with your kindness.

Second chances at love can be a blessing but also a challenge when you're trying to blend a family from two very different backgrounds and cultures. My dream of having a perfect blended family was a hope and a dream. In a time of immense frustration, I wrote:

# Illusions

Things aren't always what they seem.
It's in our illusions or in our dreams.
We want to make things right, at this moment and second, we want resolve to happen overnight.

We fail to see what is real because we rely on what we feel,
And,
We fail to see things as they are. Truth be told, we wish on stars.

Yes, things aren't always what they seem.
We want. We hope, and we dream.

We live our lives up in the clouds, voices loud.
We can't hear. We listen not. We close our ears.
If truth be told, we would rather run away. But love makes us stay.

Things aren't always what they seem.
We rely too much on our hopes, and we rely on our dreams.

*New Year's 2017*

Growing up as a Puerto-Rican in the city of Chicago was not easy, never fitting in because we were white to the blacks or "spics" to the white community. I had to find my identity in Christ, as the world was not going to give it to me, or my family, for that matter. There is tremendous pain when you live in a world that defines you by the color of your skin and not your spirit. Especially when that place is the place you call your home church.

# Pain

Why do you look at the color of my skin
As though it dictates of what lies within?

Why do you lash out with your strife? Don't we share
the same God?
Isn't he the center of your life?

Why do you scoff and stare and glare?
This should be my place of refuge and not my nightmare.

Why does your pain mean that mine is canceled out?
You have no idea of my journey or what I'm all about.

You see, we share the same blood that was shed on
the cross.
Your distain for me, while we share the same Father, is
simply your loss.

*February 2008*

Andrew met a wonderful young woman in 2010. He had never brought anyone home to meet us formally, so we knew this young lady was special. Andrew would bring Jennifer to meet us for dinner. We had them meet us at our home first so that we could break the ice before dinner. When I opened the door, there stood a statuesque, beautiful, blue-eyed beauty. We were captivated by her sweet spirit and beautiful blue ocean eyes. It was clear to me she was a daughter of the King. After dinner, Charles told me to "get ready for a wedding." He would refer to her as "a tall glass of water." Jennifer Elizabeth would become the daughter I never had. We could not have asked for a more caring, genuine, loving, and thoughtful person to marry our son.

# She's Our Tall Glass of Water

"She's a tall glass of water," he whispered,
 as she waltzed through our front door.
 She's more than we dreamed of;
 we couldn't have asked for more.

"She's a tall glass of water," he whispered,
 beautiful spirit, honest and true.
 Heart of gold and eyes the ocean blue.

Yes, she's a tall glass of water. A woman we can claim
 as our own.
A daughter that I never had, a blessing so special, who
 would have known?
That lovely glass of water stole our hearts when she
 entered our home.

2012 would prove to be a year of great transition, both good and bad. Andrew and Jennifer were engaged in January 2012. My dad passed away right after Memorial Day weekend. His health had declined for years. I had so many opportunities to tell him how I felt about him, yet I didn't. For months after his death, my mind was in overdrive thinking back on all the memories. I harbored lots of resentment toward him for many years prior to his death. However, I did forgive him and never took the time to tell him that I forgave him. It was through my own iniquity that God gave me the sight and clarity to stop holding him accountable for my life. Regret is merciless. It has no mercy because there is no going back when someone you love passes.

# The Pain of Your Passing

Daddy, I felt your embrace in a dream last night.
Your Loving arms, they held me tight.
As if to tell me your last goodbye, then I awakened,
tears flowing from my eyes.

You were youthful again, wearing your Stetson hat, hair
slicked back.
Your face aglow.
The pain of your passing ravishes my soul.
So many things about me that you didn't know.

The years flew by like a thief in the night, yesterday your
little girl.
Then suddenly, someone's mother and wife.
I never got to tell you the impact you had on my life.

The pain of your passing, it penetrates every fiber
of my soul.
I miss you and I love you. I just wanted you to know.

*August 2012*

Charlie and I decided the month that daddy passed that mom and my sister Blanca, dad's caregiver, deserved an island getaway to help them heal. We wisped them away to Puerto Rico the month after daddy passed. We stayed at a lovely resort in the city of San Juan. The evening we arrived, a salsa band was the musical treat for the night. Blanca dragged me to the floor. The immense joy and delight that she exerted while she was dancing warmed my soul. I couldn't help but giggle the entire time we were dancing because she kept turning around and around like a tip top. The music warmed her soul, it was a salve on her heart from the many, many months of helping mom care for dad. She needed this time of release in the worst way. As we sat down, she said, "Mary, how can you be sad while you're dancing? It's impossible to be sad when you're dancing." And she was right. This poem was dedicated to my beautiful sister Blanca. The joy of the Lord is her strength. Our Puerto Rico trip will always be close to my heart. We had moments of immense bonding, and I will forever hold those memories close to my heart.

# You Can't Be Sad While You're Dancing

"You can't be sad while you're dancing," she said,
  as she whirled across the floor.
  Her feet carried by the music of salsa and merengue
  And her troubles were no more.

"You can't be sad while you're dancing," she said, as she
  giggled and laughed out loud.
  Her hands clapping to the sounds of the Spanish congas,
  unaware of the staring crowd.

"You can't be said while you're dancing," she said, "It
  makes you cast your cares away."
  Yes, like sunshine after a rain or storm, it casts the
  clouds away.

"You can't be sad while you're dancing," as though
  surrendering your heart,
  to all the things that grieve you. Those things that tear
  your heart apart.

"You can't be sad while you're dancing," she said;
  she pouted when the music came to a sudden close.
  "Kick your heels up and dance across the floor, once you
  have the chance," she said.
  "Feel the music in your heart and mind and toes."

The year 2012 would prove to be the year I would want to always forget. It was a year full of loss. Loss of my father. My only child, and son, getting married, and a dear friend moving away. All the while, Charles would be away most of the year on the political campaign trail covering local and national politics of the Presidential campaign. Our marriage had been fractured due to family misunderstandings and fueled by the stress of a wedding and demanding jobs. I was at my wit's end. I was feeling alone, saddened by my father's death and feeling the emptiness that the empty nest brings. Unable to sleep one night, I cried out to God.

# Lord, Heal Us

Lord, heal these places,
tears running down our faces,
from guilt, hurt and shame.

Heal our broken hearts. From the words that cut
like a knife,
That pierce our souls and tear us apart.
Unforgiveness, pain and strife, drowning our joy in life.
Renew our minds and provide us with a fresh start.

Lord, heal our walk, our crooked gait,
for the world awaits our gifts;
place in us, a steadfast faith.

And for those who wish to divide, who harbor pride,
who dare to hate and wish demise,
We pray for your grace.

Lord, heal our places
and wipe the tears from our faces.
May your unfailing love keep us, Amen.

Andrew met the love of his life in 2011—Jennifer Elizabeth Erbland. They were engaged one year later. I was in awe of the love and respect they demonstrated toward one another. I was so content that Andrew found his love that I celebrated them with this poem:

# I See Pure Love

There are things you must see in pure love.
Their spirits emanate warmth and
You can touch the color, yellow, as though
embracing the sun
when they smile at one another.

Their love wakes up each day and gives birth to smiles
and laughter.
Their daily charge is to make certain the world smiles
with them.
Sadness, rudeness, selfishness, they are not an option
for the love they behold.

Whatever they do or wherever they go,
the colors of the rainbow follow.
God Smiles. The earth smiles.

These are the things I see in the love they share.

The year that Andrew and Jenn were married, they lost their first child early in Jenn's pregnancy. Their loss grieved them greatly, and there was nothing we could say or do to quench their grief. This poem came from my soul as I grieved with them in their pain.

# I Knew You Before I Sent You

"I knew you before I sent you," said Jesus, as he kissed
 them on their heads,
"There is no trial I haven't allowed on your road in life,"
 Jesus softly said.

 Please know I will always walk ahead of you in your trials,
 surrounding you both with my grace.
"I knew you before I sent you to your mother's
 womb,' he said,
 As he gently kisses their hands and face.
 My beloved favored ones,
 know that I am the Great I AM,
 I love you, and know, that your grief, I understand.

"I knew you before I sent you," said Jesus
 As he gently rubs their tired feet.
 There is no trial you cannot bear,
 Your love and faith in me, is your weapon for defeat.

"I knew you before I sent you," said Jesus,
 embracing Andrew and Jennifer gently in his arms.
 As he gently wipes away every tear from their face and
 softly says:
"I have never left you, nor will I ever leave you."
 "know your strength lies in my loving grace."

Andrew and Jennifer shed heavy tears over the loss of their first child. Yet, God is so good he gifted them with a beautiful baby girl in 2014. Olivia Ruth would steal our hearts. My first grandchild gave me so much joy I wanted to shout her birth from the rooftops. Her beauty has been beyond what I ever imagined. Her beautiful, inquiring, sensitive spirit provokes me to be a better person. Having this little angel in our lives gave me purpose again. I wrote this for her first birthday.

# Our Olive Tree

Olivia, firstborn of my firstborn.
First blessing of our next generation.
Black hair and blue dancing eyes.
You are stunning. You are an angelic parental combination
of heavenly perfection.

Olivia, firstborn of my firstborn. Joy invades my soul in
your presence.
I am reminded of God's love for me.
The same love I felt the day of your daddy's birth.

Olivia, firstborn of my firstborn. You're a gift to our
family tree.
I delight in contentment as our family tree is more enriched.
There resides in this tree more magnificent beauty.
My cup overflows as the goodness of God envelops my soul.

My granddaughter Olivia used to look straight into my eyes and tell me, "you have pretty eyes, Gege." Each time she would say those words, it gave me a sense of wholeness, comfort, and joy. One day, my daughter-in-law, who I choose to call the daughter I never had, sent me a text message. It was an image of Olivia frolicking in a bed of leaves. As the wind would blow and scatter the leaves about, she would chase after them in a sweet spirit of joy. The photograph captured her chasing leaves wearing a string of pearls. The image was priceless.

# Chasing Leaves, Wearing Pearls

Chasing leaves, wearing pearls,
little Olivia, our little funny girl.

Chasing leaves, wearing pearls,
angelic innocence, our little cherub girl.

Chasing leaves, wearing pearls,
she twirls and twirls, in her own little world.

Chasing leaves, wearing pearls, dancing in the daylight sun,
Dance along her little black curls,

Our little Olivia, our precious girl.

Andrew and Jenn would make some life changing decisions as they welcomed two more beautiful baby girls, Violet and Louisa. This decision would take them to Louisville, far from Chicago. This would be the first time in over thirty-three years I would not have Andrew live in Chicago. This was his home where he was born and raised, went to college at Northwestern, married, and started his family. This move would shake my life as I knew it. It would cause me to live a "new normal." While I was thrilled that he was entering a world of immense opportunity for his career, it would take my beautiful family far from me. My tribute to them:

# You Are My Heart

I know God's love for me in true form.
His Gifts of each of you.

You are my heart.
My joy.
You are my sunshine on a rainy day.
Descending his love in the raindrops,
Ascend the glorious flowers in the blooms of May.

You are my heart.
Kisses, hugs, love always growing.
The joy of God in each of you, a constant unfolding.

You are my favorite perfume, my favorite color, my favorite song.
I give God thanks for all of you, all day long.
The beautiful notes that compose a wonderful symphony,
I know God's love when he gifted each of you to me.
My heart, God's destiny for me.
YOU are my heart.

There have been many people who have influenced my walk with the Lord. However, my salvation came because I had a very persistent sibling, my sister, Olga, who wanted to see me whole. I received Christ as Lord in 1993, after a prolonged period of depression. It was Olga's concern for me and her desire to see me whole that led me to the cross. She was a constant source of support and always full of wisdom. She has been on this journey with me, and so I wrote this poem for her during a season in her life she needed to know that she still had purpose.

# Olga, My Orchid

Olga my orchid, innocent and refined,
before you were formed in your mother's womb,
I had declared you "as mine."

Olga, my orchid,
Symbol of wealth, royalty and perfection,
I am pleased with you, my faithful servant,
And you have always had my heavenly affection.

This new wine will perfect the gifts
I gave you years ago.
To bring the lost, the crippled in spirit,
And hungry to the fold.

I know your fears, your concerns, and I have seen
your tears,
And I say, fear not, Olga, my orchid.
This is your time, and I declare,
Your latter days will be more blessed than all the
former years.

Listen Olga, my precious, delicate orchid. This is the time
heaven has foretold.
I have called you to do a work, which I trust you will uphold.
I am your Abba father; I am perfecting you into
precious gold.

There is another sister, Elle. She was always my partner in crime growing up. Many people have asked if I'm the older sibling, as she has such a beautiful childlike spirit. Elle has been through many trials in her life. What we all admire about her is her ability to navigate through the trials of life with a smile on her face. Her faith is the kind of faith that moves mountains. She laughs her way through the trials that would knock others off their square. She holds on to the cloak of Jesus with tenacity and longsuffering.

# Your Faith

Your faith raises you up on eagle's wings.
Your joy is your strength, as on the cloak of Christ you cling.

You refuse to ponder the cares of this world.
God smiles down at you and crowns you with rubies
and pearls.

These jewels are a symbol of your deep love for God and
your unshakable faith.
And in return, Jesus extends to you his mercy and grace.

Jesus smiles at your sincere love for life.
He sings over you as you sleep through the night.
His song speaks of his servant, in whom he takes
great delight.

Many say I'm much like my dear mother, Alta Gracia, (High Grace). They say I "act just like her." I always take that as a compliment because I believe she is the strongest and loyal person I know. While I didn't appreciate her strength as a young teen, I grew to admire her more and more with each passing year of my adult life. She had endured great trials of lack and loss in her life, and yet her faith remains unshakable. At the seasoned age of ninety-nine, she continues to cook, sew, and garden. I believe she is most at peace in her rose garden, in which she takes great pride.

# In Your Garden

In your rose garden, you find peace,
the hummingbirds and cardinals are attracted to
Your lovely scent as they fly about searching for
something to eat.

In your garden, you find peace.
As the sunshine kisses you from your head down to
your feet,

In your garden, you feel loved.
The birds you admire so very much, the blue jays, the
wood peckers and the doves, they linger there as though
sent from above.

In your rose garden, you enter gladness.
Your thoughts are filled with hope and joy as they drown
out any lingering sadness.

In your garden, you enter God's chamber of wholeness,
when you're in his presence, there's an absence of
loneliness.

In your garden, you are at peace.

It was over twenty years ago, I was out to dinner with a group of friends. We were colleagues in the organ transplant field. Working amid the scene of constant death and suffering, it stirred them to do more with their God-given talents. As these women shared their stories of medical school, law school, and higher education, I sat in silence. I went home that night and asked God why I suddenly felt inept, as though I wasn't fulfilling my calling. I opened the Bible and there was this verse: Psalm 45:1.

My heart is stirred by a noble theme as I recite my verses for the king; my tongue is the pen of a skillful writer.

The Lord has downloaded many ideas since that time, but I've been too busy, distracted and doing life, that I never pursued my passion until now. Whatever the Lord has placed in you to do, do it as unto the Lord. Completing this short compilation of poems has given me a sense of purpose again. This is just the beginning.

In Christ,
*Mary T.*

CPSIA information can be obtained
at www.ICGtesting.com
Printed in the USA
LVHW092302020320
648805LV00001B/285